Cats Are Better Than Dogs

A Cat's Eye View

as told to Bob Lovka

illustrations by Ronald Lipking

BOWTIE PRESS

Irvine, California

Ruth Strother, project manager
Nick Clemente, special consultant
Amy Fox, editor
Liza Samala / Michael Vincent Capozzi, designers
Suzy Gehrls, production manager

Text copyright © 2001 by BowTie™ Press
Illustrations copyright © 2001 by Ronald Lipking
All rights reserved. No part of this book may be reproduced, stored in a retrieval system, or transmitted in any form or by any means, electronic, mechanical, photocopying, recording, or otherwise, without the prior written permission of BowTie™ Press, except for the inclusion of brief quotations in an acknowledged review.

Library of Congress Cataloging-in-Publication Data
Lovka, Bob, date.
    Cats are better than dogs : a cat's eye view / as told to Bob Lovka ; illustrated by Ronald Lipking.
       p. cm.
    ISBN 1-889540-62-5 (pbk. : alk. paper)
    1. Cats—Humor. 2. Dogs—Humor.   I. Title.
  PN6231.C23 L6864 2001
  636.8'002'07--dc21
                                    2001001194

BowTie™ Press
3 Burroughs, Irvine, California 92618

Printed and Bound in Singapore

First Printing August 2001

10 9 8 7 6 5 4 3 2 1

A Preface of Sorts

Change is the unchanging condition of life. Yet, we hear that "the more things change, the more they remain the same" and laments such as "some things never change." This is especially true in the world of cats and dogs. To wit: my dog, Foon, an accomplished author and Benji's ex-agent, has an ongoing battle with my cat, Sonny, another accomplished author but one too ethical to be an ex-agent (or lawyer, for that matter), over the unchanging Question of who's better, cats or dogs.

The Question results in raging arguments between Foon and Sonny, not unlike the silly raging arguments people get into over even less important questions. Their latest "discussion" prompted Foon once again to bring out pen and paw and put forth the canine view of this topic. *Dogs Are Better Than Cats* was the result. Sonny was appalled. In an effort to set the record (and maybe some CDs) straight, Sonny took to the keyboard, and traipsing over it, clicked out the marvelous tome you now hold in your hands. Citing actual case studies (so Sonny says) and plenty of opinion from cats all over the neighborhood, the case is herein made for feline superiority. That and a symbolic representation of what cats really are in comparison to dogs.

Sounds pretty scientific to me, although the science seems to be a bit prejudiced toward the cat point of view, and Foon lividly disagrees with the findings. The ultimate answer to the Question is yours to discern. I can't afford to venture an opinion; I have to live with them both, and I am a gentle, peace-loving person from Cleveland just trying to get by.

—Bob Lovka
The Feline Institute of Comparative Psychology

Cats Are	Dogs Are
Oysters on the half shell	Fish sticks
First class	Coach
Mountains	Molehills
The Three Musketeers	The Three Stooges
Antonio Banderas	Drew Carey
Wimbledon	The Bowl-O-Rama
Croquet	Mud wrestling
Fedoras	Dunce caps
Violins	Kazoos
Parchment	Recycled paper
Brass fittings	Plastic
Fourth of July sparklers	Duds
Sipping champagne from a goblet	Guzzling beer from a can

Cats Are

Arias and operas
Vichyssoise and bouillabaisse
Beowulf
Hamlet
Strawberry crepes

Dogs Are

Mimes and oompah-pah bands
Canned tomato soup
Bubble gum comics
Burlesque
Peanut butter and
jelly sandwiches

Cats are Beverly Hills.   Dogs are Beverly Hillbillies.

Cats Are

A glass of Merlot

Sherlock Holmes

Velvet

$E=mc^2$

Croutons

A decaf double tall hazelnut nonfat latte

A double-Dutch chocolate chip
raspberry sundae with nuts,
whipped cream, and a cherry on top

Cats are cuisine.

Dogs Are

A quart of Ripple
Inspector Clouseau
Burlap
2+2=5
Bread crumbs
A cup of joe
Plain ol' vanilla

Dogs are grub.

A Quick Look at History Proves Cats Have Always Been #1

There is nothing new about the natural superiority of cats. Back in Ancient Egypt, cats—not dogs—were honored and deified. The goddess Bastet, who was associated with grace, fertility, and beauty, was represented as having the body of a woman and the head of a cat. Ask yourself what self-respecting goddess would manifest herself as a dog? The goddess NOBODY, that's who.

In Egypt, cats were the cat's meow. Cat tombs, cat statues, and cat mummies were everywhere. Even the mighty sphinx was the representation of a cat. (Well, actually a lion,

but we all know what a lion is—nothing more than a cat on growth hormones.)

In Ancient Rome, the goddess of Liberty was depicted with a cat at her feet. Pretty honorable, I'd say. King Louis XV of France, Chinese emperors, and American presidents such as Lincoln, Teddy Roosevelt, Ronald Reagan, and Bill Clinton kept cats. Cats even traveled with the pilgrims on the Mayflower (dogs took a raft), and it was the cat, not the clumsy dog, that Leonardo da Vinci called nature's masterpiece. History is on the side of the cat!

And by the way, don't buy into that historical baloney about letting "sleeping dogs lie" (they "lie" all the time whether they're sleeping or not, but that's another matter). No less than the great prophet Mohammed when finding a cat asleep on his robe is said to have cut a hole around the precious kitty rather than disturb her. It's "let sleeping cats sleep," thank you very much.

And Heaven knows, there's a world of differ-ence between a sip (cats) and a slurp (dogs)!

Cats autograph

Cats interject

Dogs sign with an "X"

Dogs interrupt

Cats nibble.

*Dogs chew with their mouths open,
slobbering all over the place.*

The question has always been: Should dogs be allowed into normal society? The answer is that if you want your society to remain normal, then NO! Dogs are destructive, indecent, degenerate, and they have bad breath.

Cats never offend. Take a dog into a social setting and somebody's going to start a fight. England's War of the Roses probably started over some dog getting loose in a rose garden;

they have that effect. Cats, on the other hand, purr and calm everybody down. Look at great human achievement in a society and you'll find a cat nearby. Ernest Hemingway wrote great stories with a cat or three whispering in his ear. When dogs whisper, you get the Son of Sam.

It should be clear even to non-felines: Cats can be trusted, dogs must be watched!

Cats are Ivy League.

Cats Are

Doers
High heels
Federal Express
Eggs Benedict
Bottled water
Soup

Dogs Are

Doo-dooers
Loafers
Pony Express
Breakfast burritos
Tap water
Nuts (and how!)

Dogs are Poison ivy.

Left Brained, Right Brained, Cat Brained

Let's talk brainpower. In structure, a cat's brain is more similar to the human brain than a dog's will ever be. Cats learn quickly and adapt, are purposeful, and have great recall ability. Like humans, we are visually oriented, relying on sight to identify things, while dogs rely more on smell to tell them what's what. Take a cat to an art gallery and she'll appreciate it; take a dog and he'll sniff the frames!

In comparing the weight of the brain to the

weight of the body, cats have "larger" brains than all other mammals except for primates (do you really want to carry on a conversation with a monkey?) and marine mammals such as porpoises and dolphins (although I find it hard to believe that my lunch could outthink me). Ounce for ounce, the cat's brain is very powerful! As for a dog's brain, we're still searching for one.

Cats Are

Rolls Royces
Yachts
E-mail
Technicolor
Crepes
Mint Juleps
Literature
Fountain pens
Salsa

Dogs Are

Kiddie cars
Canoes
Snail mail
Black and white
Pancakes
Mint tea
Comic books
Pencils
Ketchup

Cats are diamond tiaras.

MISSY

Dogs are propeller beanies.

Cats think   Dogs guess

Cats wink   Dogs blink

Cats cuddle   Dogs crowd

Cats snuggle up   Dogs sprawl out

It Is So Obvious

Cats are undemanding, low-maintenance, and self-sufficient. With cats, busy owners can be gone for days and we'll hardly notice. Just leave some food, clean litter, the television remote, and Internet access—we're happy! Dogs have no idea what to do. A dog left alone will sit around with a stupid look on his face trying to construct a thought, then he'll fall asleep.

Everything you do with a dog is a chore. Ever try walking with one of those things? First of all, they need to be walked by someone ("Honey,

the dog needs to go out!"), which is as mysterious to us cats as to why human females need to
go to the restroom in pairs. Cats handle their
"walks" alone and with no supervision.

As for exercising walks, what a trip—literally!
Walking a dog means getting tangled up in a
leash, falling all over yourself, then getting
dragged unmercifully through brush, timber,
brambles, and thorns as the crazed canine
chases after a squirrel (as if he'll ever catch it!).

Dogs have no conception of your need to have some time to yourself. A dog wants what he wants when he wants it. A dog will wait until you're totally relaxed after a hard day's work, feet up, nestled into your favorite chair, engrossed in a book, or watching the climactic part of the movie you've waited all week to see on television, and then start. There's the pestering, the stare, the run to the door. And if you ignore that, the worst kicks in. The sorrowful whimper coated with guilt. Write off the movie, put down the book—so what if it's pouring rain and your shoes have holes in them, it's time to go for some kind of a walk. Heaven help you if you don't succumb. Psychiatrists' couches are filled with people wracked with guilt over ignoring a dog's whimper.

Not the way to go.

If you want a friend and helpmate, someone who will give you joy and comfort without getting you killed or into analysis, take up with a cat. Need more chaos and consternation in your life? Let me introduce you to the dog.

Cats are rainbows.

Cats Are

Soul mates
Champagne
Cable
Absolute magnitude
Saturday night
Caviar
Prime rib
Pâté

Dogs Are

Blind dates
Beer
Black-and-white TV
Absolute zero
Monday morning
Sardines
Baloney
Liver

And as for astronomical
and geological impact,
cats are the universe,
dogs are the neighborhood.

Dogs are rain.

A Passion for Fashion

Gucci might rhyme with poochy, but cats have all the style. Fashion designers want models who are exotic and sleek with the grace of a cat. Have you ever heard of a supermodel with the attributes of a canine? Are you kidding! I have yet to find a designer who wants to have

his model look like a dog. Look at shar-peis (wrin-kled and dowdy) and sheepdogs (bad hair days to the max). At the very least, cats fit properly into their skins. Cats are tailored; dogs are frumps! And what has been the dog's only con-tribution to fashion? The poodle skirt! Case closed.

Cats are Imported.

Cats Are

Folding money
Filet mignon
Saks
Refined

Dogs Are

Small change
Ground chuck
Sears
Refurbished

Dogs are Domestic.

Cats Are

Impressive

Important

Immaculate

Dogs Are

Imperfect

Implausible

Impossible

Dining Plus Dogs Equals Disaster

Have you ever tried to eat dinner with dogs around? It's not a pretty sight. The only "table manners" dogs exhibit are pounce and devour. Besides the mad dash to the doggie dish and the throwing of food all over the floor, there's the slobbering and drooling as they start, and the whining and begging as they finish.

A dog regards any icky mess you place before him as a gourmet repast. With boundless enthusiasm, the dog will dive headfirst into his doggie bowl, then shove and knock it around the house until it winds up in a corner somewhere, painting the floor, baseboards, and walls with the sloppy remnants of "dinner." Then, with great aplomb

(and slobbery goop dripping from his chin), the dog will look up at you and ask for more!

Thank your lucky stars that cats are the direct opposite. Cats are the epitome of table grace and charm—dainty bites, careful chewing, and, oftentimes, leaving a morsel or two in order to refrain from gluttonous behavior.

More quiet dinners and formal dinner parties have been ruined by the presence of dogs than can be counted on all the paws of all the world's cats throughout their nine lives. Good thing no dogs were allowed at The Last Supper—Christianity never would have gotten off the ground.

Cats are chess.

Cats Are

Special delivery
SUVs
Roses
Vintage wine
Art school
Evian and Sparklettes
Butter

Dogs Are

Postage due
Pickup trucks
Stinkweed
Cheap beer
Reform school
Bathtub and toilet
Margarine

Dogs are tick-tac-toe.

Potty Views

Nowhere is the difference between cats and dogs more clearly defined than in the matter of "going potty." Cats tend to their bathroom "business" quietly, efficiently, and daintily, never calling attention to the task at hand. Dogs, however, turn their business of "business" into a social event. A dog on the "go" will pinball from tree to fire hydrant to lawn to flower bed to open field in a manic search for "the right spot." (Unfortunately for owners, no matter where

that spot is, it somehow coincides with being in line with the owner's next footstep!) After the dog determines his "right" spot, a ceremony ensues in which he finally makes his daily deposit, then, kicks up dirt, leaves, other's "business," his own "business," and anything else not nailed down, scattering the stuff hither and yon, often onto yon owner's leg in the process. After all that, the dog meanders about ten feet and does it all over again!

Cats "complete and cover" in one nontheatrical move. A dainty deposit, a neat cover-and-bury, and off we go as if the whole silly business had never taken place.

Cats "go" quickly, quietly, and privately. Dogs relish giving an Olympian performance in front of groups. You must have witnessed something like this: a designated pooper struts in front of

his peer group, runs through a pseudo-athletic routine of sniff-locate-circle-and-squat much to the appreciation and admiration of his peers, who, most likely, are scoring the event on a scale of one to ten. To canines, this ridiculous display isn't simply "nature calling," it's big time entertainment. Do you really want to buddy up with a creature like that?

Remember:

TABBY

Cats are refined	Dogs need reforming
Cats lick	Dogs drool
Cats know	Dogs guess
Cats meditate	Dogs snooze
Cats dine	Dogs devour
Cats share	Dogs guard
Cats see the whole picture	Dogs have tunnel vision
Cats think, anticipate, conceptualize, and infer	Dogs go, "Huh?" "Wha?" and "Duh"

Cats kiss.   Dogs slobber.

Romance, Thy Name Is Cat!

Ah, "S." Cats are soft, sweet, and sensitive. Looking for a partner who understands you? Look no further than that furry friend who can read your mind. Cats are in tune with your innermost feelings and thoughts. We pick up on your mood changes and are affected by whatever you're going through. That's why cats are the epitome of romance! Cats are the gazing at ripples on a moonlit sea. Dogs are the drinking of Ripple from a paper bag. A cat is a leisurely stroll in the moonlight. A dog is a mad dash to the convenience store. Cats are definitely dineout, and dogs are supremely drive-through.

It's all in the way cats operate. We're thinkers

and poets at heart. While dogs are Mickey Spillaine, cats are Byron and Elizabeth Barrett Browning. We're not into DOGgerel, we're into CATapulting your heart onto another plane. It's a matter of class vs. crass with cats at the head of the class. Cats are crisp white dress shirts with monogrammed initials. Dogs are dingy T-shirts with gravy stains.

Dogs haven't got a clue. Cats arrive with champagne and flowers. Dogs just show up late. Cats are subtle, coy, and sultry. Dogs are as subtle as a train wreck. Cats know that romance isn't hard-boiled, it's soft sell. You take time to smell the roses, not dig them up!

Cats are Teachers.

Cats Are

Carefully made plans
Embroidery
Tuxedos
Fuzzy slippers
Sailboats
Wine and cheese
The exceptional
Lightning bolts
Authors

Dogs Are

Dumb luck
Iron-on patches
Overalls
Combat boots
Tug boats
Pizza and beer
The average
Lightning bugs
Hacks

And whereas cats
master, dogs dabble.

Dogs are students.

A Cat by Any Other Phrase Would Still Be As Sweet

Human language verifies that cats are positive, attractive, and worthwhile.

Cats are symbols for being unflappable and hip (cool cats) and stand for wealth and luxury (fat cats). Overall, we're the absolute best (the cat's meow), and physically we're gorgeous (a glamour puss). You'll find cats sitting pretty in life (in the catbird seat), and moving with grace, vim, and vigor (quick as a cat).

French novelist Montaigne, in writing about humans playing with cats, questions whether a cat is amusing herself more with you than you are with her. (We're mysterious that way.) Ernest Hemingway found inspiration in the companion-

ship of cats, living with many of them all over the world.

As for dogs, it's another matter entirely! In your human-speak, dogs are a disaster. Dogs are the epitome of things taking a turn for the worse (going to the dogs), of being in trouble (in the dog house), and for feeling ill (sick as a dog). It's a cold and vicious life with dogs (a dog-eat-dog world) filled with hopelessness (a dog's chance), lies (a dog-faced liar), and the inability to change things (you can't teach an old dog new tricks). It's enough to turn you mean and nasty (like a junkyard dog)!

Cats achieve
Cats glide

Cats are a single
beauty rose.

Dogs barely get by
Dogs trip

Dogs are a single dirty meat bone.

Live life on the bright side—hook up with a cat.

Cats Are

Top hats and tails
Formula One racing
Popcorn
Pistachios
Designer dresses
Internet entrepreneurs

Cats are the good.

Dogs Are

Baseball caps and jeans
Demolition derbies
The kernels
Peanuts
Off-the-rack
Door-to-door sales

Dogs are the bad and the ugly.

And always remember that interacting with a cat is like kissing your lover. Interacting with a dog is like kissing your brother.

And when was the last time somebody named a Broadway musical *Dogs?*

Cats push.

Cats imply	Dogs demand
Cats own	Dogs rent
Cats question	Dogs believe
Cats giggle	Dogs guffaw
Cats explore	Dogs accept
Cats know for sure	Dogs just guess

Dogs pull.

Cats Observe, Dogs Ignore

Cats are explorers, hide-and-seekers. We're imaginative, and we love to get away from it all by hiding under blankets, crawling under beds and into closets, pouncing into empty boxes, and jumping into open dresser drawers. Cats are spies and observers, and very little escapes our attention. Leave a paper bag on the floor and within two seconds a cat will be inside it. We notice every change made to our territory. Cats look, stare, creep, test, and

take charge of whatever you put into our space. Dogs, however, don't take time to notice a cruise missile in the bathtub: saying they're oblivious is putting it kindly. If it's not food or poop a dog has no idea what it is or why it's there. And when it is food or poop, dogs act

as if they can't tell the difference between the two! Leave a shoe lying around, and a dog will chew it. Throw a ball, and a dog will walk the other way. While cats check everything out, dogs trip over it all. Now, this slapstick canine behavior might be good for a few laughs, but honestly, aren't curiosity and awareness far more rewarding in the long run? It comes down

to this: Cats are aware, and dogs don't care.

Cats are mentally alert, intelligent, live in the moment, and exhibit total awareness. If a bug invades your home, a cat will notice, scout it out, investigate, and take sentry action to rid you of the pest (or turn it into lunch) while a dog will sleep, oblivious to the fact that an army of ants could be crawling across his snoring nose.

Dogs have the reputation of being watch dogs and guard dogs, but the thing they watch most is you eating dinner, and the only thing they guard are their dirty chew toys. A cat will sense someone coming to your door minutes before a dog announces the invader, intruder, or friend with mindless barks that mean only, *Hey, did you guys hear something? I think I did—well, maybe not. I dunno.* A dog will bark at the wind, for crying out loud—that's obsession, not guarding!

Cats are aware of subtle changes in your surroundings. Leave something in a place it hasn't been before and a cat will be there investigating. Misplace your keys or wallet or purse? Follow the cat! A dog, on the other paw, is going to trip over anything in his way as he makes a beeline for food or to bark at the wind. A day later he'll ask himself, "*Wasn't there something on the floor around here?*"

Since the beginning of time, cats have had to alert dogs to guard your property and take notice of their own surroundings (except for the location of their food bowls). It hasn't been easy. And we cats never have gotten credit for semi-opening dogs' eyes to the world around them. A cat will "act funny" to tell you when a

storm is coming. If you rely on a dog's awareness, you'll be standing outside looking up into a
dark sky with rain falling onto your face before
the dog gets the message.

If you must have a dog, do yourself a favor.
Employ a cat to show him around and teach him
the ropes!

PPPUUUURRRRRRRRRRRRRRRrrrrrrrrrr

Cats Are

Art galleries
Kisses at sunset
A sexy wink
Teflon
Tiptoeing
A little lick
The fairways and green

Cats are A
gentle purr.

Dogs Are

Pool halls

Barking morning, noon, and night

A vacant stare

Sandpaper

Stomping

A giant slobber

The bunkers and
rough

*Dogs are an
annoying snore.*

Of course, in the garden
of life, cats pat down,
dogs dig up!

AAAAUUGGGRRRR-BLURP

Cats Are	Dogs Are
Layer cakes	Urinal cakes
Coiffures	Bad hair days
Class valedictorians	Class clowns
Pillows	Rugs
Mysterious	Obvious
Piccolos	Tubas
Fashion and Flair	Sweats 'n Shorts
Tinkling bells and wind chimes	Cymbals and gongs

Cats are Fortune 500.

Dogs are FBI Ten Most Wanted.

Honest Emotions

Haven't we all had enough of the touchy-feely supersensitive whiners, criers, and gushers that were so in vogue in the mid-1980s and early 1990s? If you have, you'll be happy and comfortable in a loving relationship with a cat.

While a dog will go gaga by leaping, panting, licking, drooling, and oftentimes mounting any Tom, Dick, or Harriet who walks into the room, a cat displays only honest affection. Cats are not tramps, falling into every available set of open arms. Cats develop meaningful relationships over time. We're here for the long run!

How can you trust a best friend or true love whose nose finds delight with every crotch it runs into? You'll never find a cat acting so primitively! Cats are loyal and sincere. We have character and integrity. We nuzzle up to the one we love instead of leaping like lunatics at the Anyone who opens a food can.

Further, cats respect your individuality. A cat will give you space; a dog will be in your space. Dogs are all flattery, flash, and fluff, while cats are long-lasting love. Dogs are spur-of-the-moment and showy. Cats are sweet and sincere. Cats aren't out to wrangle food, praise, or a walk in the park from you. We're pretty particular about who we like, and once we bond there's no flimflam or phoniness about our feelings.

Cats don't make an affliction out of affection. We're not needy, we're truly loving!

Cat Careers vs. Dog Careers

Cats Become

Writers
Opera singers
Poets
Bakers
Chefs
Ballerinas
Race car drivers
Yachtsmen
Spa owners
Movie stars
Philosophers

Cats are artists.

Dogs Become

Sleeping night watchmen
Professional bouncers
Bank robbers
Butchers
Short-order cooks
Grave diggers
Tank drivers
Tugboat captains
Gym operators
Movie extras
Lumberjacks (anything
to be near a tree)

Dogs are fire hydrant painters.

Cats Are

"Oooh, a door!"
Calligraphy
Oil paint
Curious
Chic and glamour
Luxury liners
Domestic
Mental
Wedding cakes
Cary Grant movies

Cats are tai chi chuan.

Dogs Are

"Oh. A door?"
Scribbles
Crayons
Cautious
Bread and butter
Dinghies
Destructive
Physical
Cupcakes
Arnold Schwarzenegger
movies

Dogs are sumo wrestling.

Cats are perfectly balanced.

Cats Are

Medium rare
Lions
Quilts
Cashmere
Diamonds and pearls
Silk
Hooks and yarn
Central air
Gruyere cheese
Talking, looking, and thinking
Lobster Newburg
Si magnifique!

Dogs Are

Well done
Wolves
Blankets
Wool
Zircons and beads
Rayon
Needle and thread
Fans
Cheez Whiz
Barking, panting, and scratching
Corned beef hash
de rigueur

Dogs are perfectly clumsy.

Yes, it's a fact. Cats are refined, cultured, and physically superior to dogs!

Of Course, There's the DNA Factor

Cats and dogs are genetically as well as psychologically and physically different. A dog's DNA (Don't kNow Anything) accounts for his overall lack of intelligence, while a cat's DNA (Dynamic Natural Ability) programs her toward excellence in all her endeavors.

Hearkening back to the gene pool, cats draw upon the nobility and grandeur of ancient Egypt and the wisdom of the Orient. Dogs trace their roots back to prehistoric caves (to sleep in) and primordial forests (to lift legs in). It appears

that they haven't advanced at all since then.

Cats have developed into incredible physical specimens. Did you know that cats can hear ten octaves and can differentiate between notes only one-tenth of a tone apart? We easily recognize different sounds, from the can opener opening tonight's dinner to the particular sound your car engine makes when it pulls into the driveway. Our finely tuned hearing also appreciates good music. (Never let a dog pick out your next CD.)

Cats are also the ballerinas of the animal world. We have a variety of horizontal and vertical jumps and leaps that leave the ordinary dog confused and earthbound. We effortlessly clear five times our own height, and have a built-in balancing mechanism that helps us right ourselves during a fall or descent. While a dog falls like a ton of bricks, a cat twists and turns, righting herself to make a graceful landing. We're beautifully balanced. We have the agility to walk along the tops of fences with no problem. A dog would be falling all over himself! And you can trust us to be careful when we're walk-

ing atop your TV or up on shelves; we won't
knock things over! Allow that with a dog and
you'll be reaching for a broom and dustpan to
clean up the mess. All in all, cats are the role
models for grace, agility, refinement, and
charm.

If you want to spend all your time supervising,
reforming, and correcting, you'll just love dogs.
But if you want a true companion, an equal, a
friend—someone who's loving without being
clingy, and cute without all the drooling and
dirt, then for you, cats are better than dogs!